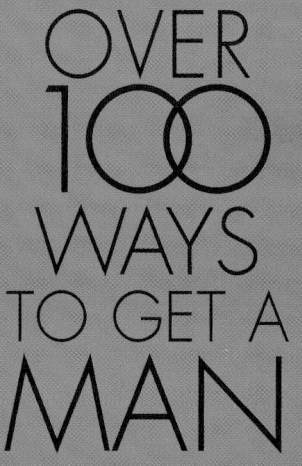

THIS IS A CARLTON BOOK

Text and design copyright © 2001 Carlton Books Limited
This edition was published by Carlton Books Limited in 2001
20 Mortimer Street, London W1T 3JW

This book is sold subject to the condition that it shall not, by way of trade or otherwise, be lent, resold, hired out or otherwise circulated without the publisher's prior written consent in any form of cover or binding other than that in which it is published and without a similar condition including this condition being imposed upon the subsequent purchaser.

All rights reserved.
A CIP catalogue for this book is available from the British Library.
ISBN 1 84222 275 9

Printed in Singapore

Editorial Manager: Venetia Penfold

Art Director: Penny Stock

Project Editor: Zia Mattocks

Copy Editor: Jane Donovan

Design: DW Design

Production Manager: Garry Lewis

The expression Cosmopolitan is the trademark of The National Magazine Company Ltd and the Hearst Corporation, registered in the UK and USA and other principal countries in the world and is the absolute property of The National Magazine Company and the Hearst Corporation. The use of this trademark other than with the express permission of The National Magazine Company or the Hearst Corporation is strictly prohibited.

COSMOPOLITAN

OVER 100 WAYS TO GET A MAN

LISA SUSSMAN

CARLTON BOOKS

Section One

When You Have Three Seconds

Studies confirm that the impression you make in the first **three seconds** is the lasting one. We make up our minds in an instant about how sexy we find the other person.

Here's what to do when you have just a few moments to grab his attention. Remember, though, while it's good to tune into your gut instincts, never put yourself in a vulnerable position with a stranger where you are on your own with him in a secluded place, and don't tell him your address.

ACCESSORIZE

Sometimes all it takes is the right prop to catch a guy's eye.

1 **Use the novel approach.** Certain books are guaranteed to put him in the mood to chat. *Fever Pitch*, *Zen and the Art of Motorcycle Maintenance* and *The Hitchhiker's Guide to the Galaxy* are all good guy-catchers.

Men are often more comfortable talking about – and to – **big friendly dogs** than they are about approaching a woman. So take your pooch – or borrow one – for a leisurely walk in the park. Bring along a toy and throw it in the direction of an attractive prospect. Or (accidentally-on-purpose) hit him on the head with your ball. That's sure to get him talking.

3

Grab your camera (film optional). When you see someone you want to talk to, hold up the camera and say, 'Fromage!'.

4

Go fly a kite. And don't be upset if you can't get yours airborne. Keep trying until you spot the guy you want to help you.

DOUBLE TAKES

Consider yourself warned: these five subtle, but totally sexifying beauty moves will inexplicably draw every man in the area directly towards you.

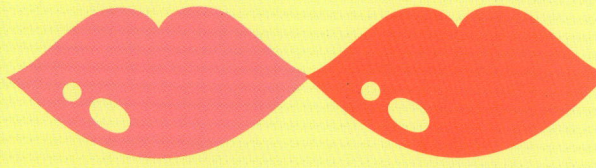

5 **Spellbind him** with lips he'll lust for. A berry shade whispers seductively, while a deep vibrant red shouts, 'Look at me!'

Tempt him to **touch you** by massaging baby oil into your skin. Go out and enjoy your new high TQ (touchability quotient) by 'accidentally' brushing your bare arm against a cute guy's biceps. Instead of apologizing, simply smile – silky seductive skin means never having to say you're sorry.

6

Captivate him with your **alluring cleavage**. While a push-up bra can make your bosom perk up, a subtle golden shimmer will make it stand out among the masses. For a stare-if-you-dare divide, smooth on a sparkling sheer liquid bronzer from collarbone to cleavage, concentrating some colour in between your breasts to create the illusion of a deep, lusty neckline.

7

Eroticize your scent. If you want your scent to draw guys in like bees to honey, avoid the number one fragrance faux pas: perfume overload. Forgo heavy scents for a subtle citrus fragrance that he'll sneak up closer to sniff.

9

Tease him with lustrous locks. **Catch his eye** with the world's shiniest coif. Rinsing beaten egg whites into your head during your shower will add instant moisture, shine and bounce.

GIVE YOURSELF A MAKEOVER

Knock-'em-out beauty is within your control.

Get a facial. Studies have revealed that the one thing that's guaranteed to make his head do a 360-degree turn is smooth, shiny skin (glossy hair doesn't hurt either). It's a sign of high oestrogen levels and difficult-to-mimic signs of youthfulness and fertility.

Dye your hair blonde. Research has found that blondes are more likely to be seen as eye candy than people with darker colouring.

Get dolled up. When a New Mexico State University study recorded beauty preferences, it was found that the look that made his eyes pop is a high forehead, full lips, a short jaw, a small chin and nose, big eyes and knife-sharp cheekbones. In short, Barbie lives.

Do your abs. A University of Texas study suggests that men prefer a 0.7 waist-to-hip ratio (i.e., the hips are roughly a third larger than the waist), possibly because it broadcasts a female's health and readiness to breed. For the record, Cindy Crawford and Naomi Campbell inch in with a 0.69 ratio. But so does anyone with a 70-cm (28-in) waist and 100-cm (40-in) hips – which just happens to be 47 per cent of the UK female population.

SCENT HIM OUT

Smell is sexual chemistry in the most basic sense of the phrase. In a recent survey by the Fragrance Foundation, both men and women rated scent as an important aspect of sex appeal, giving odour an 8.4 rating on a scale of ten.

Follow your cycle. Researchers have established that a woman smells significantly different during ovulation – the time when she is most likely to become pregnant and therefore most needs to attract a mate – and that men are capable of sniffing out this change.

15 Use a **green-apple** scented lip gloss, then move in close. The scent has been found to work the limbic or sex part of the brain.

Stub out your cigarette. People who smoke are at a considerable disadvantage when it comes to smelling the subtle scents of sex. Smokers cover up their own natural scents, too, which puts others literally 'off the scent' – not to mention ash breath, yellow teeth and prematurely wrinkled skin. Bottom line: unless you're Bette Davis, lighting up cools his flame.

Douse yourself with lavender. Scientists have discovered that just a whiff of this fragrance can increase his penile blood-flow by 40 per cent, proving it to be quite the man-magnet. Other hot scent combos include **black liquorice and doughnuts**, and doughnuts and pumpkin pie.

17

Skip the perfume. Humans produce their own airborne, 'here I am, come and get me' aromatic signals to the opposite sex. These are known as pheromones. Just stroll past and spritz him.

Around the world, **sweat** is used as a love potion. An old Caribbean recipe reads: 'Prepare hamburger patty. Step in your own sweat. Cook. Serve to the person desired.'

FOLLOW YOUR INSTINCTS

There's more to animal magnetism than meets the eye. Scientists have found that it's not that men are suckers for good looks; rather, they're genetically programmed to seek out a certain KIND of looks.

9

20

Stop dieting. Researchers at the University of Pennsylvania in Philadelphia showed pictures of female bodies ranging from almost skeletal to Rubenesque and found that it's not the men who plump for skinny women – it's the women. Biology dictates that women need a certain amount of body fat to produce hormones, periods and breasts (i.e. to produce offspring).

Go for an older guy – or **lie about your age**. According to a study of over 10,000 people in 37 countries, men are basically suckers for anyone younger than them (they equate youth with fertility).

According to the **symmetry theory** of physical attractiveness, callipers may be the only male-baiting accessory you need. It seems that humans, like most other species, show a strong preference for individuals who, when you draw a line down the centre of their body from their forehead to their toes, match up perfectly on the left and right sides. Studies have found that well-balanced babes have more – and better – sex than their lopsided counterparts. They're even more likely to have synchronized orgasms.

Look for your male twin. The reason why? Imprinting. People tend to be subconsciously attracted to replications of their parents. Hopefully they'll nurture you in the same way – only better. After years of trying to avoid becoming like Mum and Dad, we now look to date them.

24

Don't stand out. Studies show that from England to Australia and even a sprinkling of hunting/gathering tribes, the facial ideal of attractiveness tends to be very middle-of-the-road. It's thought to be a prehistoric instinct that the more average a person is, the less likely they are to carry nasty health problems that will end up infecting the gene line.

Go pulling just before your period when your **oestrogen levels** surge. This is the Marilyn Monroe of hormones. It makes you feel finger-licking desirable and more likely to be chatted up.

25

CREATE CHEMISTRY

You can't score if you're not playing the field. Ninety per cent of life is about showing up in the first place. Go out to places with signs of life – intelligent or otherwise – and use these tricks.

26 Dress like you're a success. When researchers showed photographs to a group of men of one particular woman, either dressed comfortably or wearing a business suit, the men rated the nicely dressed version to be much more appealing, without realizing it was the same woman. **Talk about a power suit!**

27

Make the first move. Ninety-five per cent of men polled said they would love to be approached by a woman.

28

A New England centre for the Study of the Family discovered that **WHERE** you meet someone for the first time can strongly influence attraction. For instance, when men met a woman in the gym, they thought she was sexy and healthy-looking. But when they ran into the same woman at the pub, they rated her as unattractive.

Get in his **line of vision** so he notices you. Ninety-nine per cent of attracting a guy's attention is about getting him to see you in the first place.

29 @ 99%

Give up. That's right, forget about finding a date. Instead, start finding out what it is you love to do and what (besides the entire male species) fascinates and enthralls you most. When you stop waiting around for a guy to change your life, Mr Wonderful is most likely to show up. Ironic, huh?

If you **go out** with a group of friends or even just one girlfriend, make sure you separate off from them so that you appear to be more approachable. No man wants to be rejected in front of a group of women, and he may well feel he cannot approach you when you are 'protected' by a herd of other women!

HEAD MOVES TO MAKE HIM NOTICE YOU

Sometimes all he needs is a nod in the right direction.

32 Toss your head. This is the classic attention-grabber. Flip your head back so your face tilts upwards. The movement attracts his eye as your face catches the light. It means: 'Hi, look at me' (usually used at the same time as tip 36 below).

33 Let him know you care with a **flip of the hair**. Raise one hand and push your fingers through your hair. This can be done once, slowly and thoughtfully, or in short spurts, pulling your hair back and drawing attention to your face. He'll think you're gorgeous and come your way. Follow this up with tip 35.

34 The head **nod** is usually done when you're passing almost nose-to-nose. Nod your head gently backwards and forwards until you're communicating by moving together in a gentle sway. It's a quick way to tell him, 'Come with me, I'm more than interested.'

35 The Eyebrow Flash is the first of what psychologists call 'the looks'. Raise both eyebrows in an exaggerated gesture, follow by lowering your eyes quickly to establish eye contact momentarily. As the eyebrows rise to their peak, the eyeballs are exposed because the eyelids lift and the muscles around the eyes stretch, allowing more light onto the surface of the eyes. This makes them appear large and bright, and very attractive. It's a genetically programmed classic come-on.

36 Tilt your head to one side and smile. You trigger a subtle sexual arousal in him by revealing a portion of your neck – even though the gesture suggests a certain demureness. (Think of Princess Di's famous head tilt and smile.) The more you tilt your head, the more you're showing your interest. Throw some lip-licking and side-glancing into the mix (see tips 60 and 63) and you'll have him on his knees.

Section Two

When You Have Three Minutes

Your next move is the one that has the power to reduce a man to a trembling wreck. It's not beauty or even big breasts that attract men – it's knowing how to play the game. Make no mistake – flirting works. There's no better way to grab and hold a man's attention.

Here are some sexy follow-up strategies for when you have a few more minutes on your side. Beware: these moves are guaranteed to turn even the biggest stud into a love-struck puppy.

WORK YOUR BODY

These body moves are sure to entice him.

Crossing your arms is a natural instinctive response when you're feeling vulnerable. The problem is, it signals DO NOT APPROACH. To avoid doing this, put one hand in your pocket, on your hip or on the arm of a chair. Or hold something like a drink or a pen (useful for exchanging phone numbers).

38

Working out is a great way to get male attention – not because you might meet guys at the gym (although you probably will), but because you will love the way a strong healthy body feels when you have the energy and ability to do anything. When you're comfortable with yourself, you inevitably come across as being more confident, sexy and fun.

Practise a sexy walk. Stand up straight, take a stride about one and a half times the length of your foot. This is the distance men are biologically fine-tuned to read as a sign of health and fertility, making you a hot prospect for passing on their genes.

39

40

When you **slide onto a bar stool**, sit with your legs crossed at the knee in what's called the Leg Twine. To wrap him around your little toe, languidly stroke your calf and let your shoe fall partly off.

Get the same effect from a distance by **crossing your legs** so they point towards a nearby cutie, showing that you'd like to enter his personal space (about 0.9 m/3 ft, according to studies).

41

NO-TOUCH SEDUCTION

Here's how to get a man to approach you without even lifting a finger.

Get a flushed face by thinking of something sexy or embarrassing. It's a signal to him that you're attracted to him.

Guys are suckers for long tresses. So entwine him in **your locks** by running your fingers through your hair and tossing it in his direction.

Scrub your tongue with a toothbrush every time you clean your teeth. Then let it slide out a little when your target is near. A healthy pink tongue is a visual turn-on for him.

45

Regular, **moderate exercise** alters metabolic rates and hormone levels, which often results in a greater sense of wellbeing and energy, an aura of confidence and an increased level of sexual desire – all powerful honey attractants.

46

When we first notice someone, we spend about **three seconds** scanning their face, flicking our eyes backwards and forwards between the other person's eyes, then moving down to the mouth and finishing off with a few broader sweeps that take in the hair. Extending the scan to four-and-a-half seconds will create strong emotions in him.

47

Buy time with a smile. Studies have found that when you smile at someone, they take a longer look because they are made to feel at ease.

HOW TO GET A MAN'S ATTENTION – ANYWHERE, ANYTIME

Now you've spotted him, here are some new, improved ways to catch his eye, start a conversation and keep it going.

48

ON THE STREET: Ask for directions – even if you live in the neighbourhood.

WHAT YOU SHOULD SAY: 'Excuse me,' which should then, in a millisecond, tell you how receptive he's going to be to you. If he seems to welcome the intrusion, ask the whereabouts of a shop, restaurant or bar.

WHY THIS WILL WORK: Men love to be helpful (and act like know-it-alls).

POSSIBLE NEXT MOVE: After he gives you the instructions, say, 'I should write this down.' At that point, you should pull out a pen and paper and scribble down the directions. This will prolong the encounter, and if he's interested, he'll wait. If a prolonged conversation starts, since you already have your pen and paper out, you can ask for his number.

49

AT A SUPERMARKET: Ask him a practical question and allow him the chance to help you out. Use the many hidden mysteries of the supermarket as a jumping-off point.

WHAT YOU SHOULD SAY: 'Do you know where they keep the crisps?' Then follow him around the aisles to find them. Or say, 'Can you reach that roll of paper towels?' or 'Can you believe how much this costs?' Or point out some snack choice in his cart (you'll have lots to choose from!) and say, 'Excuse me, but is that good? I'm supposed to bring something to a party later.'

WHY THIS WILL WORK: A direct question is always answerable and if he rebuffs you, you can always save face by asking the very next passer-by the same question (so your target ends up looking like a rude people-phobe).

POSSIBLE NEXT MOVE: More questions: 'I don't shop here that often. Is it always this crowded?' This is one step away from saying, as ironically as possible, 'So, do you come here often?' It leads to talk of his shopping schedule, which gives you information on his lifestyle (as does the contents of his cart), which can open the door to a million other topics of conversation.

50

IN A BAR: Stand near him, sip your drink and look deeply perturbed.

WHAT YOU SHOULD SAY: 'I might be going crazy, but does my drink taste soapy to you?' Hold out your glass to him. It doesn't matter if he takes you up on your offer to taste it. You've made the opening to say, 'I'm going to order another. Can I get you something?'

WHY THIS WILL WORK: It has nothing to do with talking about him, about you, or why you're both in the bar.

POSSIBLE NEXT MOVE: If he accepts your offer of a drink, comment on his beverage of choice. He wants a Bud? Say, 'Would you believe I tried draft for the first time recently,' which will launch a conversation about draft versus bottled. If he gets a cocktail, ask about the origin of its name, 'Who do you think Tom Collins was anyway?'

AT THE LAUNDRY: While fussing with a machine, surreptitiously drop a coin in such a way that it goes between the machines. Loudly express your frustration and attempt to pull the machines apart.

WHAT YOU SHOULD SAY: 'Oh no. I've lost so much money this way! I'll bet there's a fortune between these machines.'

WHY THIS WILL WORK: You've provided a conversation opener, and you've given him the opportunity to engage in a complaint-fest over the vagaries of doing your laundry. He might even figure out a way to help you get your money back.

POSSIBLE NEXT MOVE: Once you've been talking (or you're joined in an effort to move the washer), ask him where he lives. (It must be nearby.) Then you can discuss the neighbourhood, the building, favourite sports and so on.

51

52

AT A PARTY: Look over and smile. Smile in a big, appreciative way. Smile as if there's a caption over your head that reads, 'I'm having a great time and I'm so glad to see you.'

WHAT YOU SHOULD SAY: After edging towards him over the course of 15 minutes, say, 'Hello.' Introduce yourself. Be a human being about it, it's a party, after all. You're supposed to go to them to meet people and mingle, so you shouldn't be too embarrassed to actually attempt to do so.

WHY THIS WILL WORK: Everyone's awkward at a party and he'll be thrilled to see a friendly, happy face.

POSSIBLE NEXT MOVE: After 'Hello,' traditional follow-ups are, 'What brings you here?' or 'What's going on?' If he has any social skills at all, conversation should ensue. Once you've been talking for a while (say, half an hour), you can always make the 'It's pretty noisy in here' or 'It looks as though people are leaving' observation and casually suggest moving on to another venue, like a place to get coffee.

AT A CLUB: Have fun on the dance floor AND look like you are, too. Often, when you dance, you're so caught up with what you look like or who's checking you out that you forget to relax and enjoy yourself. Then exit the floor, get a big glass of water and stand near the guy you're interested in.

WHAT YOU SHOULD SAY: 'I was wondering what the view was like from over here, and, please, tell me that I look pretentious/silly/embarrassing on the dance floor!'

WHY THIS WILL WORK: A woman who doesn't take herself too seriously on a dance floor looks approachable.

POSSIBLE NEXT MOVE: He'll assure you that you dance divinely. Should mutual attraction happen, you could then say, 'Do you dance? Or do you come here just for the music?' If he wants to dance (and this is a huge deal for lots of men), he'll take the hint and ask you. If not, don't ask him, since his refusal could make for an awkward moment. And yes, we could ponder on why some guys go to clubs when they don't dance, but it's still a good place to meet women, right?

53

ORAL PLEASURES

How to sweet-talk him with pick-up lines guaranteed to work.

A University of Louisiana study found that the following phrases will perk up his ears (and other organs):

- 'Hi.' (97 per cent success rate)

- 'Would you like another beer?' (91 per cent success rate)

- Introducing yourself (88 per cent success rate)

- Put your sweater or jacket down on the bar and say, 'Can you do me a massive favour and watch this for a second? I have to run to the ladies' room.' (85 per cent success rate)

- 'I feel a little embarrassed about this, but I'd like to meet you.' (82 per cent success rate)

54

- Touch his watch and ask, 'Do you have the time?' (81 per cent success rate)

- Instead of asking him what he does, ask him what he enjoys doing (78 per cent success rate)

- If you're at a party, walk up and say, 'Could I talk to you for a couple of minutes? There's someone I'm trying to avoid.' (76 per cent success rate)

- 'What do you think of the band/food/movie?' (70 per cent success rate)

55

Seduce him with your voice. When it comes to sweet talk, the pitch in which something is said is more important than what's actually being said. A softer, lower tone can literally stroke the listener, conveying vitality and sexiness even if all you're doing is chatting inanely about the weather. This is why, 'It's so hot' can sound finger-lickin' hot when breathed in a candy-floss whisper, and like a weather report when uttered in the monotone of a BBC2 DJ.

Tell him a secret. Disclosure gets him on your side. Lean in and tell him something personal – even if it's whether or not you're happy in your job. Men are attracted to that comfortable feeling of safety, so this makes it easier for him to share as well. But don't reveal too much about yourself (see tip 81 for why).

Section Three

When You Have 30 Minutes

Flirting is the most subtle form of man-I-pul(ation) there is. But playing hard to get is an art form that takes practice. Successful flirting is all about telling the truth about yourself but not giving the whole game away.

Here are some man-baiting tactics for when you're pubbing or clubbing, or when you're at a party. And if you think they're too outrageous for you, remember: if there were no women out there who made the first move, most men would still be virgins.

STRUT YOUR STUFF

Being aggressive with a stranger is a no-lose situation. If he's already noticed you, then he's thrilled; if he hasn't, then you're only making yourself less invisible to him. These no-holds-barred moves will make him look twice (and ask for your number).

It may seem polite to leave a little room between you and the guy you're interested in, but extreme flirting is no place for politeness! **Lean in towards him** to give him the impression that you want to exclude everyone else in the world.

58

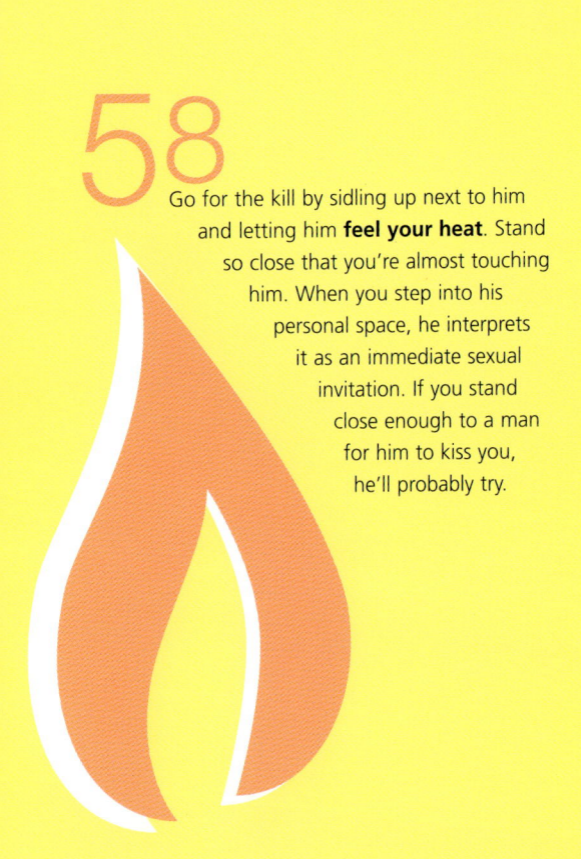

Go for the kill by sidling up next to him and letting him **feel your heat**. Stand so close that you're almost touching him. When you step into his personal space, he interprets it as an immediate sexual invitation. If you stand close enough to a man for him to kiss you, he'll probably try.

59

Stroking your lower neck can cause your nipples to become firm. He'll happily take things from there.

60

Lick your lips when you look at him. Wet lips seem to simulate vaginal lubrication, signalling that he makes you horny.

Bump into him at the bar. Then, instead of saying, 'Excuse me,' put your hand on his back. Use gentle pressure, as if he were already your lover. When he looks to see who's behind him, say 'I'm sorry, I was just trying to get past.' Then flash him an innocent smile and move on. Guaranteed he'll be right on your trail.

Read HIS body moves:
- He chews faster
- His lips part slightly as he makes eye contact
- He touches his hair
- He touches his face more, stroking his cheeks, ears or neck
- He unconsciously (we hope) points at his genitals

STARE HIM DOWN

Your eyes are 18 times more sensitive than your ears. Use them to captivate him.

The first rule men learn about picking up women is not to make an approach before they get the all-clear. One glance means a possible, 'Yes'. Two glances means, 'Come over'. Three glances and you're telling him, **'What's taking you so long?'**

Holding his gaze for two seconds is the magic number – any shorter than this and he can't be sure you're interested; any longer and he might call the cops!

Try the Two-Eyed Wink. A slower version of a normal blink, with all the playfulness (and none of the cheese factor) of a regular wink. Glance his way, then blink slowly and smile. Wait for him to smile in response, then look away again.

66

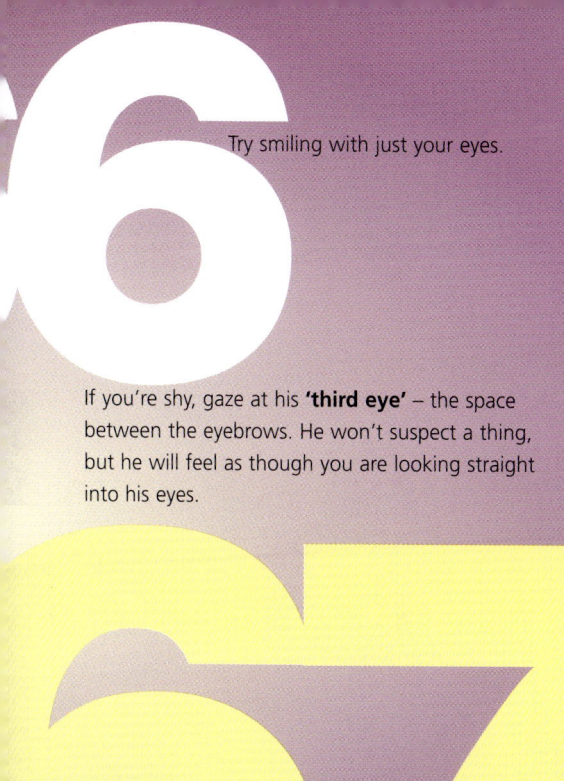

Try smiling with just your eyes.

67

If you're shy, gaze at his **'third eye'** – the space between the eyebrows. He won't suspect a thing, but he will feel as though you are looking straight into his eyes.

68

Stay in the dark. Dilated pupils send out smouldering 'Notice me' messages, even if the distension is simply the result of bad lighting.

69

Short-sighted women have a peculiar attraction for many men, possibly because their unfocused gaze seems attentive. If you wear glasses, you can get the same effect by taking them off.

BE ONE OF THE GUYS

Adopting certain guy-like behaviour will make him feel more comfortable about approaching you.

70 Know when the **hunting season** is. After scrutinizing birth records from around the world, German researchers concluded that there's a definite human mating season during the months when the sun shines for about 12 hours per day and the temperature hovers between 10 and 21 degrees C (50 and 70 degrees F). This means, biologically, you're more likely to look good to the opposite sex during these times of the year.

71

Hang out with just the guys: it makes other guys wonder why you're such a man magnet, and all that testosterone sends your flirty side soaring.

Drink beer out of a bottle. It tells him that you're down-to-earth and unpretentious, and he can be himself around you. (And that's not to mention the obviously erotic gesture of wrapping your lips around a long cylindrical object.) Cheers!

73

Ignore him. After giving him the once-over, pretend that watching paint dry would be more interesting than looking at him. It seems that while playing hard to get may be bad news for your reputation, it'll do wonders for your social calendar. Men are more often attracted to someone they have to 'chase' than someone who may be just as pretty, but more readily available. Apparently, having an urge frustrated can intensify the feeling of need, making him interpret it as must-have desire.

74

Don't leave until **closing time**. As the night wears on, magically, you become better-looking. In a study of singles-bar patrons, as closing time neared, people's judgement of a person's attractiveness increases. The reason: a psychological mechanism sensitive to shrinking opportunities. As the mating pool thins, what's left looks better and better. Of course, the next morning things may seem different!

Section Four

When You Have Three Hours

You've attracted him enough to snag a first date. Now, make him yours.

All a man really wants to know is that you like him. The trouble is, some women send out weaker signals than a cell phone submerged in water to let a man know they're interested. And if he thinks you're not into him, he'll want out of there. So, here's all you need to know to make him know that he is, without doubt, making your heart go flip-flop – without being TOO obvious about it.

DRESS FOR SEXCESS

Stylish moves that will guarantee he'll be ga-ga for good.

75

Wear something **touch-worthy**. A teasing hint of faux fur, a flirty feathered bracelet or anything else that's temptingly tactile can serve as a must-feel attention 'grab-her'. It'll catch his eye and make him want to stroke you.

Go au naturel. Using highly scented soaps and perfumes can interfere with his ability to detect your female scent, making him less likely to get turned on to you.

Get your accessories right. A poll by the University of California-Los Angeles found that guys regard a woman who accessorizes as a woman who cares about sex. The five top sexy adornments are:
* Thumb and toe rings
* Charm bracelet
* Red cars
* Red lipstick
* Black stockings

78

The colour of your clothes speaks volumes about you. Hot hues, especially scarlet, are linked with sexuality. In a study from Loyola University, Louisiana, both men and women rated red the most alluring shade, followed by dark blue, violet, black and yellow (virginal white didn't even get a look-in). Breathing and heart rates rise in the presence of strong red colours, so bright red actually makes him **physically aroused**.

Borrow his mum's clothes. The more you look like his mother or sister, the better your chances. It seems that after years of trying to avoid becoming like Mum and Dad, we now look to date them. A study from Rutgers University, New Jersey, found that people subconsciously tend to be attracted to replications of their parents or siblings in order to heal the emotional and psychological damage we all experience to some degree in childhood.

79

80

Call to him using a 'genital echo'. According to anything-that-moves watcher Desmond Morris, this alluring term covers all body parts with a passing resemblance to the genitals – in other words, a visual sexual double entendre. The belly button is one example, fingers another. (You figure out the matching genitals.) But the Big Mama of the pack is the mouth, which is thought to be a dead ringer for the vagina. In the same way as the inner labia of the vagina becomes bright red with engorged blood just prior to orgasm, our lips also become redder when we're turned on. Smearing your lips with red lipstick will send out an extra, 'I'm on the brink of ecstasy' announcement.

Wear a (figurative) **mask**. A little mystery is essential to infatuation. People almost never become captivated by someone they know well, as an Archives of Sexual Behaviour study on Israeli kibbutz marriages clearly illustrates. It was found that out of 2,769 marriages, none occurred between men and women who had actually grown up together on the kibbutz. And the reason for this? The easy familiarity of having spent their whole lives together was unconsciously translated into a chaste sibling bond instead of a passionate sexual one.

Show (off) some leg by hitching your skirt up slightly as you sit down. Or slip on a pair of high-heeled shoes, which enhances the length and shape of your **lower limbs**. This part of your body exerts an enormous sexual pull for some males. For many men, a long-legged look is dazzling, the reason being that the lengthening of the limbs is a feature of sexual maturity.

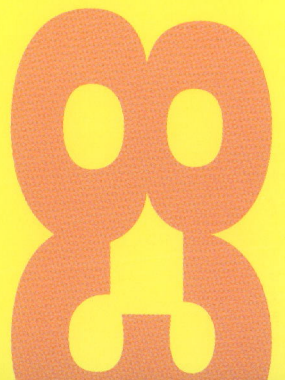

Your bottom sends out an unmistakable erotic message. Make him want to give it a pinch by wrapping it in a pair of tight-fitting jeans. You'll look like a voluptuous sex goddess.

GET HAPPY

Your mouth gives away your mood.
Make yours blissful ...

Smile only when you really mean it. A tight jaw and top lip will seem false and make your face look tension-filled and lopsided. The trick is to learn to relax your face. Practise by scrunching up all your facial muscles as tight as you possibly can for five seconds and then release them. Do this five times, then massage your temples.

84

85

Bare your teeth: both men and women tend to give open smiles when they're sexually aroused.

86

Bite your lower lip as you smile. This is a very provocative move that will make him want to lean over and give you a long, lingering smooch.

87

Smile with your mouth and eyes: this is the most friendly 'I'm-nice-to-know' smile there is. Think happy thoughts to get your face to light up. Adding a little laughter to the mix will put your body in a state of arousal similar to when you are sexually turned on and will make you seem more alluring.

88

Part your lips slightly when you smile. It'll make you seem alert, expressive and responsive. Susan Sprecher, PhD, professor of Sociology at Illinois University, conducted a cross-cultural survey of 1,667 men and women in the USA, Japan and Russia to find out what people look for in a mate. In all three countries, animation was a bigger draw than looks when it came to what made him want to get to know you better.

Giggle, but keep your mouth closed or put one hand over it so the sound is much softer. This is less intense than laughter and lets you subtly say, 'I know intimacy is on the menu, but I'm shy.'

SAY IT WITH YOUR BODY

Try some of the body moves that will make him feel at ease and connected with you.

90

When you greet him, give off a sensual and **warm aura** when you're standing, simply by resting on one foot more than the other, letting your hip jut out a bit with your hands on the small of your back.

As you talk with him, point your knees, feet, hands, shoulders or whole body **towards him** – it's a subtle way of saying that you aren't complete strangers anymore.

Women, more than men, shrink into their spaces by subconsciously tightening their bodies. To avoid this, open your body to him. **Open your hands** instead of clenching them into fists. Don't fold them in a tight hand grasp; tent the fingertips instead, and rather than sitting with your hands tightly folded, drape them loosely over the arms of the chair. Bonus: the open body represents sexy power (a closed body symbolizes weakness, insecurity or hostility).

Affectionate touching tells a guy that you like him and that you wouldn't mind touching him more in private. If he says something witty, squeeze his forearm gently and laugh. If you want to go to the ladies' room, put your hand on his shoulder and say, 'I'll be right back.'

Copy him. When two people become captivated with each other, they begin to subtly and unconsciously mimic each other's postures and gestures within five to fifty seconds. Eventually, even breathing and heartbeats become synchronized. Called 'mirroring', it's a learned habit left over from infancy when the newborn mimics its body movements with the rhythmic patterns of whatever voice is speaking to it. You can consciously use mirroring to lure him in by deliberately echoing his movements. But keep it down to less than five gestures or he's going to feel stalked. (If he changes movements every time you start copying him, don't expect him to call you again.)

Sitting up with good, yet relaxed posture shows that you're having a good time and are interested in what he has to say.

Nod as he talks to show you're paying attention, but don't do it so much that you look as if your neck is on a spring, or you will end up putting a wall between you and your date. (It's the equivalent of crossing your arms.)

97

Use your body as well as your hands to express what you mean. When you talk with your whole body, you say,
**'I'm animated,
I'm interested,
I'm interesting.'**

Section Five
When You Have 30 Hours

Enchant him, tempt him, tease him. Any guy will tell you that it's the little gestures that achieve BIG results.

Best of all, when you have time on your hands, you can s-l-o-w-l-y blaze a sizzling impression on his radar. Check out these can't-resist-you tricks and dazzle the man you desire. Use them on him and in no time at all, he'll be drawn to you like a moth to a flame.

UNEXPECTED APHRODISIACS

Not-so-obvious ploys will make him stick around.

98

Hum 'Ode to Joy'. An Indiana University study of 239 students reveals that our musical tastes can influence how hot we think someone is, and men are more attracted to women with a taste for classical music (a man's desirability is amplified by a passion for heavy metal). They're still trying to work out why, but in the meantime, pump up the volume!

99

Eat raw mushrooms: the odour is reminiscent of sex. Or just eat in front of him, period. A New York University survey discovered that most guys think that a woman who picks at her food is a total turn-off (not to mention scary – it's no secret that the most mild-mannered person will turn into an irritable monster when they are food-deprived). Having a healthy appetite makes them think that you are going to be a sensuous lover.

Practise listening. Believe it or not, just being attentive can be a turn-on for the object of your desire. Studies by language psychologist Deborah Tannen have found that women tend to interrupt more than men, making guys feel like they're not really being listened to. Keeping a little bit silent while you consider what he's saying will make you stand out because you're listening to him. And that will make him want to continue the conversation – over dinner, perhaps?

Scare yourselves sexy. Invite the object of your desire to a horror movie or for a ride on a roller-coaster. A Canadian study found that there's evidence that emotional arousal, including experiences that involve fear, triggers off sexual attraction. Research subjects who were either warned of imminent electric shock, scared to death on high, wobbly bridges or told of grotesque mutilations all tested higher for intensity of romantic passion. So did those who ran on the spot for two minutes, were severely embarrassed, or listened to a Steve Martin comedy routine.

FLIRTY FOREPLAY

Reduce an otherwise evolved man to a drooling, panting fool with these seductive gestures.

OnehundredandtwoOnehundr dandtwoOnehundredandtwo

Say his name to fan the flame. Called 'anchoring', the technique of saying his name three times while talking to him will connect him to you. Strengthen the bond between you physically by lightly touching his arm or hand when you repeat his moniker.

Use a nickname. According to a study by University of California-Los Angeles psychologist Albert Mehrabian, PhD, giving him your own private handle is a quick shortcut to making him feel up-close-and-personal with you.

PUMP UP THE PASSION

The sweet art of seduction is learning how to say, 'Come and get me' without making him feel stalked.

Check out the **material at work**. Most people select a job based on such factors as salary, status and enjoyment. But according to a study of 3,000 singles conducted by Pennsylvania State researchers, about 10 per cent of all love affairs begin between people who meet each other on the job (plus your love affair will have staying power). In another, more recent survey conducted by several temp agencies, about 2,000 career women claimed that a romance between colleagues is four times more likely to last than an affair between people who meet outside the workplace.

105

Pay a lot of **attention to his friends**. This triggers off a sense of rivalry in the guy you're after, forcing him to find a way into the conversation and exclude his buddy (never underestimate the competitiveness between men).

106

Along the same lines, **get a fake date**. If you know a great-looking male friend, by all means show him off. According to research on jealousy conducted by psychologist David Buss, PhD, there are few things more attractive to a man than the fact that other men are attracted to you. In one study, when people were asked to judge women based on photographs of them with 'spouses' of differing attractiveness, unattractive women paired off with good-looking men were routinely rated most favourably in terms of status.

107

Compete with him. Challenge him to a game of tennis and bust his balls. According to a study by John Jay College of Criminal Justice, women who don't hold back their killer instinct are seen as more attractive than those who act in a more demure fashion.

108

Cast a spell over him by throwing pink rose petals (they'll make him want to have sex) and fresh orange peel (for enticement) in your handbag or pocket. Lighting a pink candle before meeting up with him and visualizing how you want him to see you (as a sexy vixen, of course) will also influence his attitude.

GRAB HOLD OF HIM

Ways to touch him to let him know you want him – NOW!

109

If you like him and you know it, **clap your hands**. The truth is, we're more likely to be attracted to someone who is obviously attracted to us. This give-and-take element was confirmed in a University of California study of passion influences, where the perception of being liked ranked just as high as the presence of sex appeal in the potential partner.

Flex and he'll think sex. Gestures exposing vulnerable areas such as the underside of your arms, sometimes while fondling a glass or keys, or running a fingertip along the arm of a table tell a man you are ready to expose yourself to him.

Remind him of what's **beneath your clothes**. Dangle a shoe off your bare toe or let the sleeve of your top slip off your shoulder so you're just a little more bare than he expects. One of the greatest turn-ons of all is imagining the parts of another person's body that you can't see. Showing him a little skin, even if it's not the most risqué spot, will be a hint of things to come … if he plays his cards right.

112

Scientists have observed that people tend to clasp their hands behind their head, elbows pointed skywards and armpits wafting outwards when they want to send out an arousal signal. It's a way of saying, 'Look at me. Listen to me. Smell me. **I'm sexy.**' (And who's going to argue with a couple of loaded armpits?)

Give him a little smooch. A Georgia Tech University study revealed that the sebaceous glands found all over the body act as a sort of bonding agent. When two people ingest each other's sebum, usually through a kiss, they become 'addicted' to each other's chemicals, making them want to couple up to maintain the warm, cuddly feelings all the time.

113

Give him an orgasm. A University of Manchester study indicates that when a person collapses in a joyful heap of contractual ripples, their brain levels of oxytocin, a sort of hormonal superglue, rise, making them feel more attracted and attached to their lover. Unfortunately, it doesn't work the other way around – the researchers found that the degree of romantic attachment had no effect on orgasm.

Caressing his head and face will have a similar effect to the above (but it isn't as much fun!).

16

Leave him guessing. Firmly clasp both your arms around his waist for no more than a few seconds. Then leave him to work out whether that embrace was 'sisterly' or not.